Tease Book

Margaret Sullivan & Jodi Lennon

Illustrated by Tom Bachtell

CHICAGO REVIEW PRESS

The author and the publisher disclaim all liability incurred in connection with the use of the information contained in this book.

Illustrations by Tom Bachtell
Interior design: Fran Lee and Sean O'Neill

First edition
Published by Chicago Review Press, Incorporated
814 North Franklin Street, Chicago, Illinois 60610
Printed in the United States of America
ISBN 1-55652-245-2

5 4 3 2 1

For Yvonne, and also Norm
J.L.

For Norm, and also Yvonne
M.S.

Contents

Acknowledgments

Thanks to our families, Laura Spargo, Cheryl Sloan, Jay Johnston, Anthony Rosenthal, Alton Miller, The Annoyance Theater, Amy Sedaris, Mick Napier, and Stoley

Introduction

Dear Boyfriends and Girlfriends,

This collection of excellent dates was born in the bits of paper and cut-up index cards on which your humble authors have stored their little dreams of fun things to do in anticipation of the right company. Just because the social world has become a teeming cesspool of rudeness and alienation doesn't mean we all don't know better. The fact that you are holding this book in your hands suggests that you already know that drinking ice beer in a sports bar, playing video games, or watching new releases on a television screen might not be the only way to look into the soul of the one who could be your partner for all eternity.

We mean to solve the problems that occur when the hopeful romantic adolescent dreamer in you meets the defensive, boring slackers that these times have delivered up.

We also mean to reform the darkness around us that warns us not to meet any strangers, not to risk appearing silly or mixed up, not to break our concentration on our own selfish interests, not to let anything happen out of our vigorous control.

Everyone in the world deserves to have as much fun as possible. Dating seems to be the best attempt our civilization has come up with to combine our yearning for understanding and affiliation with our urge to mate. Slowly, over the centuries, we've added a few new hairdos and, of course, cars, but the essence remains. We go on dates to experience the shared happiness of one person entertaining another.

Margaret Sullivan and Jodi Lennon

Icons

Naturally, all of these dates have been tested by your authors in laboratory settings, as well as in the field—we're not saying with whom. Here's hoping these symbols offer you some suggestion of what could be coming your way.

High vulnerability—good for bonding

Good after-fight date

No brainer

Warning: logistically complex

 Absolutely free

 Warning: preparation intense

 Guaranteed to change your life

1

First Dates and Blind Dates

First dates allow you an opportunity to be anyone you want to be without fear of being challenged for acting affected. In the event that this date could lead to many others, we suggest a little mental preparation. Now is the time to consolidate your ideas about what sort of behavior you want to act out over time. Even if you have known your date beforehand in other professional or social situations, it's OK to be different on a date, because we say so.

So decide as you ready yourself whether you would like to start batting your eyes, swirling your hair over your shoulders, throwing your head back when

you laugh, or speaking in an exotic and ambiguous accent.

* * *

Spend your entire first date planning your second date, in case you decide to go on one.

First dates can be so intimidating. You may find yourself saying things like, "It is so unlike me to trail toilet paper from my shoes" or "I almost never have food in my teeth." But if your date requires nothing more than planning a date, then you are hardly responsible for much more than seeming to be an interesting person with fascinating ideas. And you can steal those from this book.

Have a five-course meal one course at a time in five different restaurants.

Be sure to go home after each course and change your clothes. You and your date can take turns picking each other up. Having five mini-dates in one evening will give you a big jump on your relationship.

Pretend you are tourist-adventurers in your own neighborhood.

Walk slowly, stare at building cornerstones, and photograph the graffiti. Say "Pardone?" in an international accent when people speak to you.

Go to a grocery store with a tray of tiny crackers spread with cheese and offer free samples to everyone until the management asks you to leave.

Getting rejected together will insert you both in an instant club. We suggest that you buy the cheese and crackers at the same grocery store, go to your place to make your tray, then return as host and hostess.

Write predictions about whether or not you and your date will be together in six months.

Seal your forecasts in one envelope to be opened together six months later, no matter what. Don't forget to sign your names across the seal.

Have a long conversation about things that are really, really nice.

Discuss subjects from this list only:

- Little, tiny bunnies rescued from bad people
- Warm, soft blankets
- Heart-shaped boxes of chocolates
- Ponytails strung with ribbons
- Thick, clean, white towels
- A wicker chair in a flower garden

Interview one another at length about old girlfriends and boyfriends.

Ask for evidence in the form of pictures, presents received, and letters in case they're lying.

Open a checking account together and use it as a date fund. Then, go around trying to write temporary checks for your date activities.

Spend half an hour agreeing with each other about everything and half an hour disagreeing.

After every sentence your date utters, you get to say, "Oh, but I must differ" or "Gracious! You are right on target again," depending on what time it is.

Go to a religious service that neither of you is familiar with.

Religion was once a form of theater, so why not go to the latest show in town?

Go to extremely crowded sporting events or bars, get separated on purpose, and then try to find one another.

This will produce good first-date information. You'll get to learn how your date reacts to finding you again. Be advised of a possible unhappy outcome here: your date doesn't recognize you, is with another date, or has run home.

Interview people as if for a feature story on the end of the world.

Be sure to practice this line in advance: "Thank you, I think we've got enough."

Pawn something in exchange for an instrument you can't play.

Meet at a pawnshop; any one will do. You both need to part with a relatively valuable item. If it's not that valuable, make up a heart-wrenching story as to its origin. This is a good time to check out your date's bargaining powers. Make sure you're always in control of the situation. Ask to see the special items in back.

Start to play all of the instruments you can get your hands on. Insist on tuning them all. Tell the salesperson that you and your date have perfect pitch, and it's a good thing you came in.

Once you and your date have acquired your instruments, you must name them, like all the greats did.

Make up story characters, then go out looking for people you would cast as those characters if you were making a movie.

Why not join everyone else who is writing a screenplay? And this project is free from budgets and censors.

Looking for the perfect actors is an excellent excuse to stare at people. If you want to go all the way on your first date, you can tell people you are a casting/director team and interview your prospective talent on the spot. Anybody will talk to you if they think you're in show biz.

Offer to drive high school students anywhere they want to go.

Wouldn't you have wanted a ride with someone as cool as you when you were in high school?

Go to a courtroom trial.

Why watch "Court TV" when you can sit just feet away from an armed robber, a prostitute, or a perpetrator in a domestic dispute?

After the trial, be sure to initiate an interesting conversation on the judicial system.

Donate platelets and watch a free movie.

Here's what we call quality time. Don't worry if you're the squeamish type, because passing out in front of your date will result in never-ending empathy and concern for your well-being.

Practice hearing each other's confessions and forgiving your date.

Dating is only one way that we can keep the "nobody's perfect" laws in effect. And first dates present the best possibility to get the skinny on your date before he or she gets a chance to turn defensive. We recommend making up a long list of sins you've committed, even if they're not true, because your date may try to top them by divulging some real dirt.

Visit a sex education class at a local college.

Make prank phone calls to each other's bosses.

Stage a screaming fight in a crowded public place, like a ticket line at a movie theater.

This date might not be so funny later when you have real content in your fights. If you try this activity before you know each other, you needn't worry that you'll accidentally say something you really mean. Have your date shriek this at innocent bystanders: "Do I seem selfish to you?"

Watch each other eat sloppy foods, like tacos or chili dogs.

Drop change and see who picks it up.

We recommend about twenty dollars' worth of quarters. Let's face it, that's a cheap date. Your own coffee can of pennies will work in a pinch, though. The toughest part of dropping change is making sure no one sees you. So be quick. You and your date could use a hide-out. The old trick of sitting on a bench behind a newspaper could work; you can peek around to see who's picking up your rewards.

Crash a sales convention meeting.

You and your date can have your own private circus. All you need is a "Hello My name is . . ." sticker. Decide in advance whether you'll be having the Chicken Kiev or the fish. Or, better yet, call ahead and demand a kosher meal for diabetic vegetarians.

See if you can each spend ten dollars—fifty cents at a time.

This means you can visit one of those surreal dollar stores, since you can pool your allotments for things that come two in a package, like the yellow and red plastic containers for mustard and ketchup. You now have made a domestic purchase together, a real leap for a first date.

Get a roll of quarters and find areas where police officers are writing tickets, so you can run ahead and fill the empty meters.

We have found that on first dates most people like to boast about their humanitarian side and their generous and politically aware spirits. This activity will get your dates to put their money where their mouths are.

Make rockets out of aspirin, vinegar, and Alka-Seltzer.

All you need is some open space and the absence of a child-proof cap. In time, your natural instinct will be to aim them at each other. You'll both discover an adrenaline rush similar to that of a soldier in battle. But all's fair in love and war, right?

Play golf in the snow with tennis balls.

2

Group Dates

Hi!
Hi!
Hi!

The group-date activity is optimal in the authors' minds because it discourages the nasty confrontation one-on-one daters must face eventually: the possibility of a relationship. You can go on twenty group dates in as many nights and never have to deal with the questions, "Am I getting too involved?" or "Should I inquire about my date's sexual history now or later?"

Group dates should communicate to bystanders the impression of a loosely threaded mob with a common goal. People should cross the street when they see you coming, partly because they're confused, but mostly because they're envious.

Find out when they turn on public water fountains at the end of the winter season and assemble there to receive the first gush.

Of course, this is an event that requires its own song, which you will have to compose. We recommend that round-style technique where everyone sits in a circle and contributes a line of your song in turn. This should be fulfilling for those in your group date who never had poetry workshop day in their high school.

Visit symphony rehearsals.

If this were a date for two, everyone would think you were posing for some liquor ad or, worse yet, just trying to be special. In the group-date format, however, it will appear that your group has been invited for a particular reason.

Give each other manicures.

While it takes a group to create a salon atmosphere, it only takes two to have those extra special manicurist-to-client conversations. This group date gives you that group feeling, but it also allows for the intimacy a manicure can offer.

Go see the head of a major corporation and complain about how they treat the workers.

This date presents another wonderful opportunity to name something, in this case, the workers' support group you represent. One of you should pose as press, adding that extra sense of urgency. Others could be appointed to generate a rush of enthusiasm among the employees that you have, at last, arrived to improve their health care coverage and to extend their vacation benefits.

Do mall-intercept interviews to discover how satisfied people are with what they're wearing.

Go on color dates.

Do only orange things. For example, eat Cheet-Os, purchase orange Slurpees, dine at an International House of Pancakes, then watch the sun go down.

Do blue things. For example, make blueberry muffins with your jeans on while listening to Muddy Waters tunes. Then go out and mail some letters.

Do red things. Make spaghetti sauce and cherry Jell-O, then dye everybody's hair red while you make and exchange valentines.

Fly to Chicago and eat at the Star Top Cafe.

Go on a group shoe-shopping walk where you visit ten stores and each try on a pair of shoes in each store.

No buying permitted. This date is best with a very large group.

Try to find a ghost.

No problem. The ghost needn't be visible or speak to every single member of the group. This date could be organized in a series of evenings: Ouija night, automatic writing night, cemetery night, scary-places-in-general night.

Raise funds to help find a lost dog named Pirate.

The name Pirate should unearth the repressed rogue in anyone. Bake sales are OK, but we recommend Dog Walk-a-Thons, where your patrons agree to sponsor you on a cents-per-mile basis as you walk dogs. Once you have amassed your tiny fortune, place it in an interest-bearing group account until a dog named Pirate actually does go missing.

Build a clubhouse and keep all the girls out.

Create a cable access television show where each of you interviews your mom about the day you were born.

Rewrite the last paragraphs of fairy tales. Then offer to babysit your friends' kids and glue the new endings into their books while the kids are sleeping.

Invent new beverages and name them after yourselves.

No fair with Dr. Cranberrypepper. This is your chance to dignify your family name forever.

Take stuffed animals to a Unitarian church and ask the caring minister to bless them.

Decorate your cars and have a very loud parade.

If you've gone on the Apply for All the

Licenses You Can Get Date (see chapter 7, "Testing-Ground Dates"), then you probably already have a parade permit. Be sure to synchronize your radio dials to the same skull-pounding station. Women get to wear elbow-length gloves and wave.

Solve one anothers' problems.

Everybody gets to have two. If your friends can't help you solve at least two of your problems, then: (a) they're not your friends; or (b) they're not really problems and you should forget about them.

Demand that everyone in your group write and deliver a ten-minute speech called "Why I Am So Great."

Make furniture and art objects out of garbage, then interview one another for features in decorating magazines.

Apply for jobs at fast-food restaurants.

We hope you make it to trial training. What could be more fun than swirling that puffy ice milk into a frail little cone or retorting, "Any fries with that?" The real reason for recommending this date is that you get to see your friends try on uniforms. Here's where you might get romantic ideas. If you find someone who can look good in a Pizza Hut ensemble, you may want to move over to the "First Dates" chapter.

Drive around suburban neighborhoods and find the best lawn ornaments. Then pose as the Chamber of Commerce and award the winning family with coupons for free movie rentals and manicures for the lady of the house.

Buy six dozen donuts and have your group donate them to a police station.

3

Moving Friendship Into Romance Dates

We don't know anyone who hasn't had this problem at least once. How can you get someone who sees you as a buddy to see you as the ruler of his or her future dreams—without risking the friendship? Getting them really drunk is good, but here are some dates that will situate you two in warm, open realms of possibility.

* * *

Build a Japanese teahouse together and have dinner in it.

It's best to build the teahouse before you become romantic. If you wait until your souls have caught fire, you'll just get into a fight during the planning stage.

While you're still just friends, decide on a location. We think a garage is perfect, but your bedroom could work, too. You will need new clean cardboard for walls and to make a low table, excellent paper to use as a table cover, and lots of pillows. Make your own wall hangings out of bamboo rods and rice paper that you have scribbled ambiguously on, and pretend the scribbling means something important in Japanese.

A preparation date could also include visiting a sushi restaurant and stealing one of the photographs of varieties of fish for your table. The freestanding ones encased in acrylic are optimal. You could stop at a Japanese gift shop and buy tiny little dishes for soy sauce. That process alone can bring your activities to a romantic conclusion. Just having someone buy us something creates a spontaneous sexual reaction.

Your dinner itself can be yet another date. Our research demonstrated that most teahouse establishments play Abba and REO Speedwagon, but you may want to play traditional Japanese music for atmosphere.

Walk up to strangers and shout, "Hey, you were my psychiatrist once!" Then describe several of your sessions as they try to get away from you.

Eventually, you will detect a pattern in the stories your partner creates. These, of course, are actual fears and concerns that your date has transferred into this aggressive storytelling format. At the end of the date, be sure to confront your partner with your new insights, and you will be rapt in quasi-intimacy and codependent love.

Pay for everything you do together with two-dollar bills.

By using twos, you have created your own symbolic nation with its own currency. People will begin to treat you as a unit, and, in time, you will confuse this as your own desire to be that way.

Follow a stranger all day long and take notes.

The plot lines of most cop shows and action adventure films lead us to believe that the shared experience of "casing" someone is a sure path to true intimacy.

Sneak onto a docked boat and make out.

Here's an adventuresome lure to get your date into a situation where, let's face it, there's only one thing to do.

Get your portraits taken at Sears.

You and your date should meet at Sears (preferably one in a mall), each dressed in a youthful ensemble. Neither of you can ever go wrong with a sailor suit. During the shoot, insist on holding the bunny or the big red apple. Ask for the double exposure prints that give the front and side views in one image.

When ordering prints, get lots of wallet-sized ones so you can make cards and valentines for one another later, with messages like "2 good 2 be 4 gotten."

Cut each other's hair.

We think of this as the trust walk of the nineties. Your date will now be partly responsible for the way you look.

Trade laundry and go on a Laundromat date.

If you're not well acquainted enough to fondle each other, you can fondle each other's clothes. It's almost as good and certainly safer.

Make up a romantic ceremony for moving the clocks ahead in spring.

Play albums backward in search of satanic messages.

We happen to know that bands insert evil secrets in their songs all the time. This date provides an excellent excuse to sit together in the dark.

Leave a fish in a bowl on someone's doorstep, then wait in hiding for them to come home.

Copy the behavior in a movie.

Eat when they eat, laugh when they laugh, make out when they make out. We recommend *La Femme Nikita* or *Cry-Baby*.

4

Hump Dates: Good Third or Fourth Dates

The dates that follow were designed to help you struggle out of that awkward dating adolescence—the point at which you almost don't have serious stomach pains in the presence of your date, but are not truly yourself yet. Think of these dating opportunities as springboards launching you into a state of revelation and openness that only the hippies dared to dream of.

* * *

Go through each other's things and help them get rid of clothes they don't need.

Here are some rules:

1. You don't like it.
2. You never wear it.
3. It's trashed.
4. It's ugly.

This is a great way to get to nose around your dates' belongings before they get to know you so well that they start hiding their stuff.

Go to the Salvation Army (or wherever you donated your things in the previous date) and find out how much they're charging for your old clothes.

Apply to health clubs and ask for a sample workout.

You might get interviewed together, and you can then find out what it's like to be a couple. That could get your date all embarrassed in a way you may find adorable, who knows? It's also great to get to see someone you don't know very well just out of the shower.

Form a fan club for someone who doesn't get enough attention, like Peter Tork, the forgotten Monkee.

Now you and your date have a mutual purpose that could outlive your entire relationship. Besides, your date's sensitivity to underdogs may actually inspire your increased loyalty. Once you have chosen your target fan club idol, you can develop the press kit. Research his or her life history for stories that you can manipulate into something that would interest the media. Having grown up in a huge family is charming and adorable now, whereas when your idol was being launched the first time, it was probably considered embarrassing. Also, T-shirt technology has come a long way, so you'll want to design a new one.

Be sure to choose someone you would both like to meet someday, because as president and CEO of the fan club, the two of you are bound to create enough guilt and responsibility to be flown out to meet the object of so much creative attention.

Tell each other the scariest stories you know, then watch cartoons and eat popcorn until you've forgotten them.

Photocopy the Constitution and hand it out to people on the street.

Fix all of each other's broken things and mend each other's torn clothes.

At the third-date stage, you need to introduce the concept that you are, among other things, a job, and one that your date should start taking responsibility for. Getting this date accomplished early means your relationship had some value, even if you don't continue it.

Watch TV in a department store.

Unless you met your date at Thanksgiving and were disturbed enough to invite that poor person for dinner with your family before going on the Hump Dates and Testing-Ground Dates outlined in this book for your convenience and protection, then this is probably the first opportunity you will have to feel like your date is a member of your family.

Standing awkwardly in front of a television set should send both of you into a reverie of childhood memories. And the fact that you are in public makes it all the more surreal.

Make out every time you say a word with a silent letter.

We recommend you arrange this date on a Wednesday in February, during which you have a conversation about things you should do more often, unless your date pronounces the t in often, in which case you should break up right now.

Slide across a gym floor with your socks on.

Yes, that's right.

Volunteer for scientific experiments, especially those where you are required to sleep with a lot of equipment on your head.

Here you get to see what your date looks like asleep without having to really be sleeping with them.

Go to the airport together and act like you haven't seen each other in years.

This is a good way for you to get to kiss and embrace repeatedly without being conspicuous. You'll make a lot of people happy, too. You need to move from gate to gate and hope that you manage not to do this in front of the same people more than once. You can use this date as a testing field for pet names you might be considering. For example, at Gate A, one of you could say, "Muffin?" and the other, "Soda Pop?" Then at Gate B you could try, "Fieldmouse?" or "Is that really you, Donkeyshoes?"

Build a kissing booth in a parking lot and earn lots of money.

Nothing will revitalize your interest in your date like the potential to feel attacks of jealousy. Watching your date kiss hoards of strangers will remind you of his or her attractiveness, in case you're starting to forget. And there's nothing like a jealous surge to confuse you into thinking you could be in love.

Stand outside the stage door of a theater and exclaim to everyone who exits, "Congratulations! That was the best performance we've ever seen in our whole lives."

Make perfume out of vodka and flower petals.

5

Ask Margaret and Jodi

We now interrupt our gust of glorious opportunities to address a number of urgent matters that are absolutely sure to arise in your dating life. Some common concerns are posed here in the form of questions whose urgency you will recognize from your own experience. Yes, you are welcome for the tremendous relief you will enjoy now that somebody has finally demonstrated the courage to answer these questions.

Q. How can you get someone you just met interested in dating you?

A. By being beautiful and interesting.

Q. Is it appropriate to talk at great length on a first date about operations you have had?

A. Yes, of course, and don't be selfish with the details.

Q. Should I inform my date if I have relatives who are incarcerated?

A. Only if one of your dating activities includes visiting them.

Q. How much information about my victimized childhood and the dysfunctional and abusive authority figures in my life should I share on a first date?

A. As much as possible; it gives your date the opportunity to do the same.

Q. Does dating shorten or lengthen your life?

A. Do we seem like doctors? Consult your physician.

Q. Is it a good idea to date someone just to exploit his or her social or professional connections?

A. Only if you know how to correctly pronounce and spell both their first and last names.

Q. How can a person say "I want to date you" to another person without resorting to such a bland expression of interest?

A. By coming up with a list of 200 or more things they can do on a date.

Q. Under what circumstances is it acceptable to cancel a date?

A. Only when you're sleepy.

Q. What if I bump into someone I'm dating while I'm out on a date?

A. Invite one of the workers at the establishment you are visiting to go home with you.

Q. Is one supposed to cut a hamburger in half before picking it up?

A. No, it is the french fries you must divide into four even sections.

Q. How can a man invite a woman on a date when he does not know her or anyone who can introduce him to her?

A. By staging an accident in which the woman is led to believe that she injured him seriously.

Q. When dining out, if the host asks the woman how many are in her party, should she answer?

A. No, she must stare vacuously until the problem is corrected.

Q. What if, when my date arrives, I see that I am terribly overdressed?

A. Say that you just got home from another date, and excuse yourself to change.

Q. Is it possible to be on a date and not know it?

A. Yes. We've been on lots of dates we don't know about.

Q. How many people in America are having a great time on a date right now?

A. Two, and they are on two different dates.

Q. How can you tell your date that you don't like what he or she is wearing?

A. Say, "Gosh, you look just like you're a newscaster!"

Q. If your date has food on his or her face, must you tell?

A. No.

Q. What if your date has big wet spots on his or her clothing? Do you have to say something?

A. No.

Q. Should you reapply your makeup in public?

A. Yes, every five minutes or so, lest your date think you don't like the way you look.

Q. What if your date has a distracting mannerism?

A. You should say, "Care for more eye twitch, I mean coffee?"

or "Some may find your twittering nostrils repulsive, but I am mystified."

Q. Should I change my hair color before every date?

A. Yes, that's a good idea.

Q. Do I have to join my date's religion if we go steady?

A. What do you mean by going steady?

Q. Do men resent women who do most of the talking on a date?

A. There are men who might be happy to be relieved of the burden of carrying the conversation, but we have never met them.

Q. What do you do if you want to end a date early?

A. Summon a police officer.

Q. What about problem personalities, I mean dates who you really like personally, but who are so eccentric that they embarrass you in public?

A. You should dress as your date's nurse or paid companion, so that people assume you are really good at your job.

Q. What if I don't like my personality?

A. Going on lots of dates will distract you from your own shortcomings.

Q. What should I say at the end of my date?

A. Go like this: "Thanks for the date."

Q. What if you are getting ready for a date, and you just don't like how you look?

A. You need to start the whole preparation process again, beginning with washing your hair and including a second set of brand-new underwear.

Q. How long is it appropriate to keep your date waiting while you finish getting ready?

A. That depends entirely on the statement you feel like making at the time. No time at all if you mean to say, "I respect you a great deal." One hour and fifteen minutes if you mean to say, "My time is extremely valuable, but yours isn't worth anything."

Q. During a date countdown, I get very nervous in the last ten seconds before arrival. My friends meditate as part of their date preparation process to overcome the anxiety of being stood up. Do you recommend this?

A. No. We recommend a date countdown that includes ten minutes of planning a strategy of vengeance if your date blows you off.

6

Meet-the-Family Dates

Before we tell you what to do when you meet the family, let's review what you should not do, because that can be just as important.

1. Try not to scratch furiously.
2. Don't use the first meeting to inquire about their wills.
3. Use a glass. If you must drink out of a bottle, remove the brown paper bag first.
4. Avoid lurking by the window, parting the blinds slightly, and peering out every minute or two.
5. Don't call the parents Gram and Gramps until the second or third date.

6. Leave your chemistry set at home.

If you can manage all this restraint, we think you're ready to meet the family.

* * *

Invite your date and his or her parents to dine at a restaurant with a clear view of a nursing home.

This is the perfect date for keeping overbearing parents in line. If you've been warned by your date that Mom and Dad can be a little controlling, you need to show them who's boss right away.

Create a photo session where you force your date's parents to pose for you.

Go to your date's parents' house, but bring along at least five children you claim are your foster kids.

Bring your date's family a case of canned goods under the pretext that you have worked on the product's advertising campaign.

Insinuate that their disloyalty to your wax

beans and pumpkin pie filling is disloyalty to you. Keep bringing them replacement cans, so they can never have fewer than twenty-four.

Invite your date's family to dinner at your place, but turn your heat up as high as it will go.

You can run your shower all day and boil large pots of water for several hours, too. Tell them all to wear shorts. You can distribute plastic leis and Singapore Slings at the door.

Engage your date's family in a lively, high-stakes game of craps.

Sign up all the members of your date's family in book and record clubs.

At your first encounter, distribute their membership cards and inform them that they'll soon be receiving their first installments, but that they can feel free to return them for any reason at no cost. And they can cancel at any time. Your date's mom might appreciate an enrollment in one of those clubs that sends you a different collector's plate every month.

If the time comes that your families meet each other, have a family circus where everyone has an act.

Your own mom and dad might make a good lion-and-tamer duo. Let your siblings be little poodles dressed like elephants.

Bring a lifelike newborn doll to meet your date's parents, and ask them to hold it for you.

Have a family taste test of cigars you must all smoke. Have them fill out surveys afterward evaluating aroma, smoothness, flavor, and style.

Go on a breakfast date, but insist that the parents pick you up at church.

You'll want your date to advise you about which church to wait in front of. Be sure your timing coordinates with actual activities. Later at breakfast, order coffee only. You've had about enough pastry after spending the whole night getting ready for the bake sale.

Get your parents to spy on your date with you.

It's OK to tell your parents that you're not quite ready to introduce your date to them, especially if it's the truth. Recommend that you and your parents drop in on your date at work or someplace where your date is likely to be—in this case, leading a sing-along in a local prison.

Pick a funeral to drop in on so you can tell your parents that the deceased was your date's best friend in the world.

Rescue pets from an animal shelter.

Balance all your checkbooks together.

Get your date to pose as someone who is repairing something in your apartment when your parents are there.

You can then ask how they like your date and get the real truth.

Agree to meet at a bowling alley.

Now your parents think of your date as a bowler, so any interesting qualities he or she might possess will come as a tremendous relief.

Get your date to come for dinner at your parents' wrapped in bandages.

Casually mention that your date was on volunteer fire-fighting duty the night before.

Arrange to have your date's parents meet you in a coffeehouse where you appear to be translating large Sanskrit documents.

Say it's for the government. They'll never know.

Write your date's parents a lengthy, obsequious letter thanking them for bringing such a wonderful person into the world.

Have a turnabout evening where you get to be your date's parents, and they become your children.

Have conversations like this:

Your date's dad: "Golly, I'm hungry!"

Your date: "How about some boiled carrots?"

Dad: "I don't think so."

Your date: "You don't sound very hungry to me."

Check into a hotel room and tell your parents that your date lives there.

Bring dozens of pictures of yourself from your whole lifetime to your first visit to your date's family's house. Suggest that they put them in their albums.

When you get together with your own and your date's families, have all the women change the oil in their cars and all the men clean the kitchen.

Have a dinner where everyone in your date's family has to wear a bandanna.

Then look up the colors in a gay guide and tell each family member what the bandanna color they have chosen means in the gay community. You can explain, "Mr. Shanley, you have a hunter green bandanna in your right pocket, which means you're a 'daddy's boy'" or "Mrs. Shanley, you have a fuchsia bandanna on and that means you're a spanker.'"

Have your date's parents take compatibility tests that you have saved from magazines.

Create a tradition where you agree to speak only in Pig Latin whenever you are all together.

7

Testing-Ground Dates

Although you may, rapt in a romantic moment, promise never to judge your date, we know better. In fact, we think it's part of your job to observe whether or not you're having fun. Remember that you are testing not only your date's worthiness but your own ability to have a wonderful time.

Lie out in the sun with a portable cassette player and a party-mix tape.

Part of your date will be scouting the perfect driveway to lie in. This is a very high vulnerability date for you because most of your primitive musical tastes will be exposed, as well as much of your body. The pay-off is in the excellent insight you receive about your date's reaction to your party tape. What you want is not tolerant acceptance but the unbridled enthusiasm of a soul mate.

Get free CPR training.

Watching your date orally stimulate a life-size plastic doll will give you an instant character profile and provide plain old good information. If you don't get to sit in a classroom very often, this is a good forum for passing romantic notes, and who cares if you get caught?

Cook a meal on a car engine.

Neither of the authors was interested enough to research this area properly. However, we did see a "Simpsons" rerun where a police officer fries eggs on his engine. We're guessing they were delicious. People who claim they can perform this sort of trick are giving their dates an important opportunity to see if they can live up to their own standards.

Go to a city or town hall and apply for all the licenses you can get.

Here is a way to engage in long, fascinating conversation without sitting in expensive restaurants. Just wait in long lines in public buildings instead. If your date is going to get testy or condescend to city employees, you need to know as soon in the relationship as possible. Having matching fishing licenses can be the inspiration for future dates, to say nothing of your marriage license.

Make a comic book together.

Your dates will certainly use the superhero model to express their innermost needs and expectations. Beware of partners whose main characters have been love-ravaged fools, psychically contained in their own superheroic desire, unable to find a kindred spirit because their own greatness is too much to understand.

Try to hypnotize each other.

The urge to cheat will be overwhelming, so this is automatically an essential test of character for you. Of course, you will want to appear to be hypnotized well before you actually are so that you can discover your date's intentions. So think of this date as a testing ground for you.

Trade apartments for a day.

If you plan to continue to date a person, you will eventually have to face how you feel in his or her living space. We think a good experiment is to remove the emotional obstacle of your date's physical presence. This is also a test of how much you trust your date not to call lots of people in foreign countries on the telephone or to read all the mail in your storage room, interpret your laundry, listen to your phone messages, or count your shoes.

See who can catch more quarters off their elbow.

For some, the results of this contest are enough. Proficiency in fifth-grade waiting-for-the-bus activities could be just what you are searching for. For others, the freedom to look stupid in front of someone you would like to impress is a valuable quality for the long haul.

Try to make each other cry by telling the saddest possible stories.

Crybaby types are easy to manipulate, so it's good to find out early if you've got one on your hands. We're thinking you might want to avoid someone who can't be penetrated at all, though. Be advised about your date's ability to leave you sobbing.

Take a hearing test together.

It's only a matter of time before one of you accuses the other of being a poor listener. Why not find out if there is any real basis for that? And you can't beat the chance to watch your date wear huge headphones and hold up two fingers every few seconds for no apparent reason.

Look at catalogs together and pick out the best item on every page.

That's right. You are what you buy, and you want to be what you want to buy.

Watch your date go through your wallet and backpack or briefcase.

You'll learn a lot if you notice the way your date handles your stuff—gruffly or not, critically or not, with respect and tenderness or not. If they love you less after a glance at your driver's license photo, they're not your friends.

Make pancake animals.

As you well know if you have read Margaret's earlier books, *Kitchen Angst* and *Cook as I Say, Not as I Do,* cooking style represents the total personality. Preparing any food together is loaded with symbolic representation of your date's whole life, as well as the lives of his or her ancestors. We chose pancake animals because they are supposed to be fun, but require some complex negotiating around the frying pan. You might ask your date, "If you were a pancake animal, what kind would you be?" Remember that if your date is belligerent or bossy at pancake animals, what sort of shrewlike behavior can you expect with something important, like pomodoro sauce?

Make New Year's resolutions for each other.

Here's where you find out what your date thinks is wrong with you. But if you've been dating defensively, you can always say, "What do they know?"

Have a party and invite all the people you suppose will be coming to your funerals.

Here's a fun way to find out whether the central people in your lives are going to be able to get along well. At some point in the festivities be sure to announce your criteria for the guest list.

Read the Bible out loud on a train.

Buy a disposable camera, then ask twenty-four strangers to take your picture. Use the photos and words cut out from magazines to make an album of your relationship.

Ask people if you can do their jobs for a little while.

Maybe your cab driver would like a little bit of a break, or you could get to tear movie tickets in half. It will be informative for you to see your date perform a variety of duties, and you can observe how comfortable people are with giving your date authority.

8

Post-Date Survey

Dating is confusing. You may ask yourself, "Did I have a good time, or not?" This is a pass/fail test to help you answer that question clearly, without leaving any room for that meaningless "gray area."

We recommend taking this test every ten minutes until you force your responses into the answers you are looking for.

If you are able to answer "yes" to any of these items, you have automatically failed.

1. Did my date use any of these expressions:

    damn straight
    tubular
    How's things?

2. Was all my hair in exactly the same position when I returned home?
3. Were there undefinable wet spots on my clothing?
4. Was my inclination to destroy the page in my calendar that recorded my date?
5. Have I picked up any new nervous habits, such as rocking back and forth in my chair?

Regardless of the previous results, if you answer "yes" to any of these items, you have automatically passed.

6. Have I been skipping?
7. Does every song I hear on the radio make me want to run to the music store and buy it?
8. Do I lie in bed and stare at the ceiling?
9. Do I want to change the beneficiary on my insurance policy?
10. Am I currently writing a stupid poem?

9

Anniversary Dates

Anyone who has been to high school can fabricate an image of the sort of person who is good at recalling trivial dates: first kiss, first mention of sex, first fight, etc. While we do not condone this, we do recognize one favorable feature of the anniversaries issue: one learns how the other celebrates things. This can't be emphasized enough. What if your date is a shriveled-walnut-for-a-heart stoic who can live without weddings, funerals, birthday parties, and christenings? We feel you need this information revealed to you in a timely and nonthreatening way. Choosing an arbitrary but cute anniversary will provide you with an informative model of your date's

approach to ceremony and gift giving. You might well think of anniversary dates as a variation of testing-ground dates and observe your date's willingness and enthusiasm accordingly.

* * *

Go to the highest point in your area (climb a hill or take an elevator) and scream out your goals in life.

Given the profusion of slacker types in our sociological midst, it is possible that your date will have nothing to say upon reaching the summit. We recommend something like: "I'm never having my electricity shut off again!" or "I'm reading nothing but pre-1840s novels for the next eight weeks!"

Go to the library and find newspapers from the day you were born.

After all, your anniversary is a celebration of you and the whimsical fact that you met at all.

Attach notes to helium-filled balloons and set them free.

How about offering the secret of your mutual happiness in a one-line statement? You could then share it with whoever fatefully receives the news.

Bake and decorate your anniversary cake.

Wash each other's hair.

If you need an anniversary to celebrate, you could choose this one. Call it "The First Time We Ever Washed Our Hair."

Go to McDonald's in your old prom and bridal party clothes.

Wear overalls and swing on a tire.

Go to a church boxing match.

Since neither of you will be equipped to prefer a favorite, this could present a treasured experience where you both could be in agreement about the outcome. Decide in advance, on the basis of the fighter's name, who is going to win. Then remember this date as the one where you both were rooting for the same side.

Draw your family trees.

Begin your own archeological dig.

Choose a location that you suppose will be protected from construction for a while, like a public park. Bring your own toothbrush and magnifying glass and start in. We think it's more creative to bury your own stuff than to find other people's gross stuff. How about storing your resolutions for the future of your relationship signed and buried at a marked spot? You could write promises to each other and come back in a year to see if they came true.

Make up a creation myth and start a new world religion.

Walk along a starlit beach holding hands.

Frankly, this one was suggested by one of our mothers. We tried going on this date, and we found it excruciatingly tedious.

10 One-Hour Dates

or

"Don't Hate Me Because I Only Have an Hour"

Some readers may think that one hour is barely enough time to get ready for a date, much less go on one, and we tend to agree. Nonetheless, we offer one-hour dates to support our belief that all the world is a date, and that there are a lot of reasons to call people and get them out just for a little while. One-hour dates are perfect for workaholics who can get full date credit for a mere one-hour commitment. Those who feel abandoned after such a brief interlude can always go on two or three of these dates at a time.

* * *

Take a walk and make a map of your trail.

Normally, map reading is the road to your first big fight, but you've only got an hour, haven't you? Be sure to make a map that fits on eight-and-a-half-by-eleven paper, so you don't need to have a discussion about how to fold it. This is a good date for showing off your art supplies if you have good ones. You'll seem so elegant and well prepared.

We recommend conceptual maps as well as actual ones. For example, you could be taking a walk anyway, but be making a map of your romantic future together, with important points like where new sheets are purchased, favorite restaurants, your own apartments, intended vacation spots, etc.

Flatten change on a train track.

Go on blindfolded trust walks.

We sure hope you attended one of those progressive high schools or junior colleges where these things are the order of the day. If not, you can recapture your lost development in creative emoting by blindfolding your date and leading him or her through a series of sixties-style sensual experiences, like a warm caress, a gentle breeze, the soft flow of a water fountain, or a big slimy bowl of wet grapes. Isn't reality fantastic?

Roller skate in a parking garage.

Order a pizza from a phone booth and wait for it there.

You may wonder how you and your date would fare in a living arrangement that isn't exactly spacious. Here's an excellent model experience. Be honest. After forty-five minutes, is your date getting on your nerves? Does your date keep going back to the question, "I wonder when the pizza's going to come?"

Go to the end-of-the-line bus depot and watch them wash the buses.

This presents a vicarious opportunity for you to discover your date's cleaning habits, which will become essential if your relationship becomes serious. Does your date exclaim, "Wow, he missed a spot!" or "Why do they have to wash the buses so often?"

The person who would ask the latter question will, in time, shove a tableful of random items into a drawer and say, "Well, the living room is all straightened," while the person who asks the former will be separating the stamps with flowers on them from the ones with flags because they can't stand seeing them in the same compartment.

Make rubbings of sewer tops.

Follow fire engines.

We recommend a picnic lunch enjoyed in a car just outside the firehouse. Bring a little something for the Dalmatian. You won't feel like waiting for more than an hour, so let's hope something big breaks while you're there.

You and your date could be the ones who say that special sentence that lures the cat down from the tree, or you might get to hold the big net the victims leap into.

Open the hood of your car and sit in traffic.

You'll discover that the world is teeming with automotive experts. Practice a few phrases like, "We think she's overheating" or "Looks like a linkage problem here." Relax in your seat while good neighbors tool around in your engine. It's a lot like getting your shoes shined. Pick your favorite among the good samaritans who stop to offer their help. You can then give that person the impression that he or she fixed your car when you start it up again. Howl with gratitude.

Write angry consumer letters to companies that make products that disappoint you.

Whip rocks at abandoned buildings.

11

Showing-Off-as-a-Couple-Dates

Truly happy couples may not get the urge to show off too often. As they drift in the sea of the dateless and the disappointed they may like to control their mirth to avoid inspiring frustration and envy in others. Who are these people? We don't know. We suppose that anyone who is having the best time in the world on a date has certainly earned it in some way and deserves world recognition, especially if they're with someone more attractive than they are or are driving an excellent car.

Tour banquet rooms and plan a big event for someday.

Be sure you and your date are dressed for the part. You may need a variety of ensembles to accommodate your choices, especially if you're going to the Elks Club and the Four Seasons on one date. Here are some questions you may want to ask the manager:

How many people can fit in the men's room at one time?

Do you allow livestock?

Can we design the waiters' uniforms?

Remember, not all banquet affairs are happy occasions. Why not plan a wake or a benefit for a disaster victim?

Buy condoms and a pregnancy test at a drugstore and make out at the counter.

Dress up as if one of you is pregnant and the other is the proud father.

People are naturally drawn to pregnant women, so this is a great conversation starter. And pregnancy gives you an excuse to get as graphic as you like. You'll surprise yourself with the number of primitive and earthy superstitions you will be able to describe. Remember to be conservative when you dress up. If you make yourself too big, you'll have the reverse effect of calming people down.

Be guest speakers at a high school career day.

All you have to do is convince the guidance counselor that you are for real. Anybody can do that. Be sure to mention your date as often as possible, confirming for high school kids that your boyfriend or girlfriend is disproportionately important.

Tell everyone you're on your honeymoon.

If your date includes a Bobby Vinton concert, you'll get a spotlight and applause. At the minimum, this ploy is good for excellent restaurant seating.

Find troubled teens and give them advice.

There's no such thing as a teen who isn't troubled, so the scouting should be easy and fun. Showing off your togetherness to a high school kid could give you the confidence you never had when you were in high school yourself and didn't have a cool date to parade around.

Attend a live taping of a talk show and make an example of yourself, no matter what the topic.

If your date deserves national attention, here's the most expedient choice. Be prepared to have overwhelming past-life flashbacks, envy your mom because she looks younger than you, forgive your cheating spouse, or have just killed your whole family. Your date can sit beside you, patting your hand and backing you up all the way, no matter what you've done.

Test drive new cars.

What an intense relationship you must be in to take such a big step. That's what your car dealer will be thinking. You might wonder, "How low will he go?" And you get to find out, too, because you have absolutely nothing to lose. Why rent a car when you can drive around and be seen in almost anything on a showroom floor?

Create surprise parties for each other and pretend you didn't know.

What an adoring couple you are! The more trivial the reason for the party, the more magnificent your date will seem for having thrown it for you. You can do the invitations yourselves in secret: "A Surprise Party to Congratulate X on His New Bike!"

Have two parties so each of you can perform both the role of the enthusiastic host who gets everyone to hide and the unwitting guest of honor.

Rent an exotic pet for the day.

What a fascinating couple you'll make wearing tree frogs and iguanas on your shoulders.

Tour condominiums for sale and act like you're buying your first home.

Great opportunity for you and your date to focus tons of attention on your "living needs" and your basic "lifestyle components." If seeing closet space excites you, then you're in for a big time. Practice saying, "What a wonderful apartment!" to each other beforehand.

When your touring needs are fulfilled, one of you should call your real estate agent and describe a sordid and seamy breakup, which should terminate any further sales calls.

12

Reenactment Dates

Just because your authors are made of dating ideas doesn't mean we have to invent every single one. Some perfectly wonderful dates have already been gone on. We suggest you borrow from that world of dates that are already parked inside the univeral consciousness. We have assembled a list of groupings that you and your date can reenact, using your own imaginations and, of course, costumes. After all, for all the help dating offers in getting to know a person, you might as well pretend you're other people. That's what we all do on dates, anyway.

Angel Clare and Tess of the D'Urbervilles

Cupid and Psyche

Dennis Hopper and Isabella Rosselini in Blue Velvet

George and Martha

George and Lenny

Harold and Maude

Mia Farrow and Frank Sinatra

Theodore and Vincent van Gogh

Han Solo and Princess Leia

Lolita and Humbert

Andy Warhol and Edie Sedgwick

Your parents on their first date

Sid and Nancy

Rob and Laura

Annie Hall and Woody Allen
(You'll both need baggy pants.)

Adam and Eve

Any two people in any Bruce
Springsteen song
(We like "The River.")

Jack Kerouac and his mom

Robin Hood and Maid Marian

Lady and the Tramp
(Do the spaghetti thing.)

Trixie and Norton

Mork and Mindy

The Beatles and their wives (group date)

Ernest Borgnine and Ethel Merman

Betty and Veronica

Leopold and Loeb

Laurel and Hardy

The Swiss Family Robinson (group date)

Jerry Lewis and Dean Martin

Anthony and Cleopatra

Eva Peron and Che Guevara

Miss Piggy and Kermit

David and Angie Bowie

Albert Einstein and Marilyn Monroe

Beauty and the Beast

Dante and Beatrice

13 Last Dates

While the authors recommend premeditated breakup dates as the most civilized, we still are exhilarated at the notion that all over the world, people are on their last dates right now and don't even realize it. Not all dates can lead to a lifetime of tedious fulfillment, and you must be elegant about the way you terminate your dating program when the time comes. Remember that the more last dates you go on, the more first dates you get to go on.

Create an act and take it to a nursing home.

We know it's depressing to break up, but it isn't as depressing as being in a nursing home. And entertaining others as your last gesture will mean that your union had some real value. Good parting memories, too.

Put flowers on people's graves.

Watch your date get dental work.

Check into a hotel room and watch TV.

Here's a good time and a way to find out whether or not you'll be able to stay friends. If you're like us, you'll remember breakups by their location, which can spoil a perfectly nice place. But what's the likelihood that you'll be checking into a hotel in your own city and get the exact room twice?

Ride horses in appropriate English equestrian gear.

If you want to be remembered as aloof, elegant, and powerful, this is the way to go.

Speak in a foreign accent all night long.

This way you won't feel so much like you are breaking up with the person you have been recently getting to know, but rather with his or her exotic foreign cousin.

Try doing stand-up at an open mike.

Just get up there and make fun of your date. Maybe you can get him or her so angry that you won't have to initiate the breakup conversation.

Be the other person for a night.

This is your opportunity to give your date a demonstration of everything you dislike in him or her. You get to mimic their voice just like you're in a real fight, too.

Write a "personals" ad to solicit your date's next target. Here's a handy phrase list to help you prepare your 25-word entry:

Master's degree or equivalent

Enjoys Mahler and Pearl Jam too!

Likes soft ocean breezes

Pulls her own weight, but likes to play with Barbies sometimes

Slow and easy afternoons to share with a special someone

Certified aerobics instructor

Accountant who can samba

Distracting your date into a new and more brief relationship will relieve you of the classic burden of shoveling your date around socially in the post-dating phase.

See if you can get a government grant for having been in your relationship.

Your breakup could serve to help others if you only had the financial resources to publish the results of your mutual discoveries. And if all you learn from your relationship is how to write a grant proposal, you'll be wiser than most people.

Drive around looking for fountains and make a wish in every one you find.

About the Authors

Margaret Sullivan is director of advertising studies at Columbia College in Chicago and the author of two cookbooks, *Kitchen Angst* and *Cook As I Say, Not As I Do.* Jodi Lennon is an actor and writer who appears in the sketch comedy show *Exit 57* on Comedy Central.